Boot Camp for Christian Writers

6

Four **More** Articles Editors Love and How to Write Them

"Writing and Selling the How-to Article"
"Finding Markets for Newspaper and Mini-Columns"
"Breaking into Magazine Markets with Fillers"
"Seeing the World—Writing the Travel Article"

Carolyn Tomlin

About the lighthouse on the Front Cover

According to legend, Peggy's Cove, Nova Scotia, Canada, was named after Margaret, a young girl, the only survivor of a ship that ran aground and sank in the 1800s. The locals started calling her "Peggy," and her home became known as "Peggy's Cove." The original lighthouse was built in 1868. Massive granite boulders line the coastline.

Lighthouses were constructed to remind sailors of a rugged and dangerous coast. On a dark, foggy night, a light from the shore offered a beacon of hope.

Lighthouses remind us of God's light in a dark world. "...I am the light of the world. Whoever follows me will never walk in darkness, but will have the light of life" (John 8:12).

Four *More* Articles Editors Love and How to Write Them
by Carolyn Tomlin

Author Website/blog: www.carolyntomlin.com
Book design: Ellen C. Maze, The Author's Mentor www.theauthorsmentor.com
Cover Image and Select Interior Photos Credit: Carolyn Tomlin

ISBN-13: 978-1480216655
ISBN-10: 1480216658

All scripture was utilized from the New International Version (NIV) Bible translations unless otherwise noted in the text.

PRINTED IN THE UNITED STATES OF AMERICA

Endorsement for the *Boot Camp for Christian Writers*

My name is B. Coyne. I have a Ph.D. in Behavior in Organizations and I am a researcher and an author. Briefly, this is my Boot Camp story: Everyone has a story locked deep within them. Denise George and Carolyn Tomlin can provide the steps necessary to bring the writing out and then to craft and re-craft it until it is publishable. If you pay attention and do the things they show you – good things happen. God worked through them to aid me in getting my work written and published.

B. Coyne, Author
Treading Water on Ripple Creek Farm: Lily

———————

Seeing "God" Through People
Carolyn,
I just wanted to thank you once again for a wonderful class today. I have already ordered the Christian Writers guide and I am anxiously awaiting its delivery. I can hardly wait to scour through the pages in anticipation of finding a magazine that will graciously provide me with an assignment.

I believe that I have some great articles and maybe even some great books inside me that are just waiting to be released! Thank you for "speaking" to my soul. I have been "writing" down ideas since I left the workshop today. Your travels, motivation, work ethics, and overall desire to do what you love are an inspiration to us all. I pulled up the "Invisible Woman" clip on *YouTube* again. It is an awesome story.

Today you talked about "writing people letters" just to say thank you. I am starting with you.

Thank you for all that you do and thank you for allowing me to be a part of "seeing God in people again."

Tara Talley
LifeLine Ministry Resources

Carolyn,

I think about our walk each time I post a picture. God guided you into my life at the perfect time for me to "get it." You, too, have blessed me so very much. Your ministry to women has been a watershed in my life. Thank you for being faithful in what He has placed in you to share with others.

Diane Bailey, Author
String of Pearls

Dear Carolyn,

I am planning to go to the March 3rd Seminar and look forward to the tag-team approach that you and Denise use. I enjoyed the other Seminars also. The Boot camp is a terrific idea and I am pleased that you both work hard in sharing it.

Student and budding author,
Tom Horton

(By attending our Boot Camp for Christian Writers, Tom Horton realized his dream of publishing a book, Adversity to Triumph, *on his family history. Although Tom was very ill, he continued to attend our Boot Camps. An encourager and loved by us all, he passed away in the summer of 2012. We honor him by setting up a Boot Camp for Christian Writers – The Tom Horton Scholarship in his memory.)*

Boot Camp for Christian Writers
Carolyn Tomlin

Four, More Articles Editors Love and How to Write Them!

Section 1
"Writing and Selling the How-to Article"

Used in both the Christian and secular market, the How-To Article is considered one of the easiest to write. Let me show you how to write about what you know, find a solution to a challenge, or share an easier way to solve a problem. Use quality photos to sell your How-To craft article ideas to editors by showing the materials needed, the steps involved in the directions and the finished product. Learn how to write in a sequence of steps, and give readers confidence in learning new information.

Section 2
"Writing Newspapers Articles and Mini-Columns"

Your local newspaper is a source for writers. Newspaper articles and short columns run anywhere from 300 to under 1,000 words, with 750 being an average. Keep your eyes and ears open to events in your community. Stay ahead of what is happening and offer to write an article. Editors need *mini* columns to finish out a column in magazines and newspapers. You can supply these needs by writing "tight" and "bright" articles that are geared to the audience and magazine.

Section 3
"Break into the Magazine Market with Fillers"

Do you have an amusing anecdote? What about a child's cute saying? Or, can you supply a brief quotation that matches the tone of the publication? Let me show you how to find these markets that use brief fillers and mini columns. I'll explain how to: Listen to conversations. Observe people. And come up with original thoughts that can turn your words into entertainment or *laugh lines* that bring smiles to readers' faces. Used for both the Christian and secular magazines.

Section 4
"See the World—Write the Travel Article"

Painting a visual picture of people, places, and things, and making readers want to go there, is only one reason to write travel articles. And the other reason? *Traveling free—or almost!* Personally, I have written dozen of travel articles while touring the U.S. and foreign countries. And most of the time, the published articles paid for the trip! You'll learn how to contact an editor before you leave home, steps to follow after returning from your trip, how to search for an unusual twist to well-known sites, how to use quotes from famous people from the area, and the value of using a *photo package* to gain the editor's attention. You'll also discover how one location provides *spinoffs* to a number of salable articles. And don't overlook *armchair travelers*—these people that want to read your articles, but never leave home. Enjoy this fun and exciting way to use your talents as a writer.

Bonus!

To make writing easier, I've included some examples that will answer questions on working with editors. Also, this book has exercises to complete at home that will improve your writing skills. The exercises are designed to be completed by yourself—or you can use them with others who enjoy this craft of writing-to-publish. Additional pages provide space for personal thoughts as you learn from this book. The Appendix offers advice as you write-to-publish. I ask God's blessings on you as you write articles that inspire, educate, inform and entertain your readers.

I believe that writing is a gift given by God. He gives us this talent and it's up to us to learn the mechanics of putting words on paper. A Bible verse that has given me hope follows:

"But those who hope in the Lord will renew their strength. They will soar on wings like eagles; they will run and not grow weary, they will walk and not be faint" (Isaiah 40:31).

"Whatever you do, work at it with all your heart, as working for the Lord, not for men… It is the Lord Christ you are serving."

~ Colossians 3:12-17 & 3:23-24

Dedication

This book is dedicated to my husband, Dr. Matt Tomlin, who has been my best critic and friend, as well as an encourager in my writing ministry.

A Personal Note to My Reader

This workbook is written especially for you—the **Boot Camp for Christian Writers**® boot campers. When you attend our all-day workshops, we are limited in time and cannot cover all the material you need. Corresponding to the workshop title, these books provide a deeper and more advanced study of the chosen topics. Designed to be used at home and when you have time to reflect, these books are a follow up to this seminar. After each section, space is provided for you to interact with the information. Use the additional pages to develop your own ideas by following the examples and format.

Writers can reach millions of readers annually through magazines. Writing can not only change the life of others—it changes your life, also! Our Boot Campers are people just like you. Perhaps you've thought of writing for years—but haven't started. Or, if you're like me, I thought no one would want to publish my work. Young people discover that writing can lead to interesting careers. Single parents earn extra money in this stay-at-home job. Seniors write their memoirs. And others turn an avocation into a vocation. You see, writing has no age limit. There's no retirement until "you" decide it's time to quit. An editor really doesn't care what you look like—or if you stay home and work in your PJs all day, or even if you comb your hair!

I've often said, "When the Lord knows it's best for me over there, in heaven instead of this earth, I hope someone finds me at my computer with my index finger on the "Send" key of my computer. And that my last manuscript "did" go through!

It is my prayer that writing will do for you—what it has done for me. And that you will develop a passion for writing and write articles and books that make a difference in the lives of others. May God bless you as you write for Him.

~With all my best wishes, Carolyn Tomlin

Table of Contents

Introduction: Starting a Writing Career in Magazine Writing

"Nothing in the world can take the place of persistence. Talent will not; nothing is more common than unsuccessful people with talent. Genius will not; unrewarded genius is almost a proverb. Education will not; the world is full of educated derelicts. Persistence and determination alone are omnipotent." ~Calvin Coolidge

I'm often asked this question: How did you start writing? What did you do first? Are there secrets you would share with beginning writers?

In this introduction, I'll share with you what worked for me. Beginning later in life, I realized the dream of writing-to-publish. Once I made this decision, there was no turning back. I was driven to pursue this goal of marketing my work. If God opens the door and gives you opportunities—you have an obligation to do your part. Realize these are personal approaches to writing. They may not work for you. I've never seen these items suggested in writers' magazines. But they work for me. And, they'll work for you, too.

Rule No. 1 – Find a quiet place to work.

Some people may consider this a weakness, but I work best in a peaceful, quiet place. My only concession is background music—instrumental only. If words are sung, I find myself listening to the artist and my mind wonders away from my work. And the music needs to be at least a room away.

I have a friend who completed his doctoral thesis on the kitchen table with 3 young children and a dog playing chase around the room. Not me! I would be a basket case!

In addition to quietness, I need my desk and room to be as clutter-free as possible. Just like I can't go to the kitchen and prepare a meal if cabinet tops are cluttered—neither can I go to a desk piled high with papers. When I see order on my desk, only then do I become creative and write.

Rule No. 2 –Discover a Different Slant

Travel writing appeals to me. Therefore, when vacations take me to new locations, I look for a different slant for travel articles. For example, take the city of Birmingham, AL. Using a keyhole approach, I take a site that offers great appeal, but one that hasn't been written about in the magazine where I plan to publish. The city of Birmingham has given me articles on botanical gardens, the children's museums, higher education, church windows and sites unique to this southern city.

And how do you identify a particular slant? Read back copies of the magazine. Use spin-offs or recent articles for new ideas. For example, you're writing for a city magazine and you notice last year's edition had an article on a new hospital. Write a query that serves as a follow-up to the hospital article where you interview physicians who have moved to the city to work in this hospital. This tells the editor you researched the magazine and you want to add additional material of interest to readers and advertisers.

"It's one of the most beautiful compensations of this life that no man can sincerely try to help another without helping himself."
~Ralph Waldo Emerson

Networking with others is one of the most powerful tools writers possess. I once heard a speaker use the analogy of the people in their life as the parts of a tree. Comparing this to the relationship between editors and writers could go something like this: The *twigs* are the secretaries, the person who answers the phone, and often the copy editor. Often these are younger people, those who are starting out in the editorial business. Someone from the twig group may give your article a "first reading" and pass it on to the editor or stamp a rejection on the cover page. Next, we have the *branches*, which include editors and assistant editors. These are the people who make the decision to offer a contract or to ask the secretary to write a rejection letter. They are important. Treat them well. We know that twigs and branches must be attached to a trunk or else, they won't survive. The *trunk* is the publishing company. If their publication is to survive, they must offer the reader articles that inspire, educate, inform or entertain. If the company receives negative complaints concerning the magazine, the editor's job is in danger. Lay-offs may occur. Down-sizing comes next. This affects everyone in the company.

Each has a role and is important to the total. Twigs gain experience and move up. Or, they relocate to another company. When a twig leaves one company and goes with another, keep in touch through email. Let the branches (editors) know you want to be part of the team and will produce articles that are in accordance with the magazine. And your article will be one that readers will respond to in a positive way.

Rule No. 4 -- Look for beauty all around you.

Train your senses to search out the beauty and good in everyday life. It has been said you can count the apples on a tree, but you can't count the seeds that will produce trees. When you write an inspirational article, it's impossible to count the people who will be changed by that article.

Beauty is all around you. Look for beauty that comes from God's earth instead of things constructed by man. Have you ever watched lighting making zigzag formations across the night sky? Do you see the honeybee as it flits from flower to flower gathering nectar that is turned into honey? Have you smelled the first drops of rain after a long, hot summer drought? What about a newborn calf's first wobbly steps? Or witnessed the tenderness in a couple's eyes as they celebrate a 60th wedding anniversary. These things bring beauty to your writing. Make these experience your own. Make them personal and weave them into your writing.

Rule No. 5 – Keep Your Day Job

In talking with new writers, my advice is this: Keep your day job. Yes, I've read of writers whose first book made the *New York Times* Best Sellers List. But in reality, that's very rare. Like other things in life, you have to pay your dues. For me, starting with the magazine market was the easiest way to break into the publishing market. Little by little, I added new magazines and networked with editors. For several years, I wrote and published 300 articles annually. That is a **lot** of words!

My suggestion is this: make writing your avocation. Then one day, after you've put in enough years to retire, write full time.

Rule No. 6 – Learn to Deal with Rejection

Rejection is part of life. When you first start submitting articles, expect rejection. Yet learn from it. If an editor takes time to make a personal remark on your paper or electronic submission—take this as something positive. Follow up with another query. And thank the editor for reviewing your work. Sometimes it takes several tries, but persistence pays off if you follow the guidelines.

Rule No. 7 –Become an "Idea" Person

Do you know what editors need from writers? They need ideas. After the editor has been with the same magazine for years—perhaps they've covered every subject they think connects with the audience. But you—the writer—can give them new thoughts and use your creativity to see a different perspective on the same subject.

Rule No. 8 –Learn the Language

Like any profession, writing has a language all its own. For example: What is a "Kill Fee?" What is "Work for Hire?" If an editor says our magazine has a "Lead Time" of 6 months, do you know when the article should be on their desk?

So where will you learn the vocabulary used by writers, editors and publishing houses? By staying in touch with other writers, attending writing workshops and reading magazines that focus on this profession. If you can't find the answer, check with a seasoned writer or find a glossary with these terms.

What You'll Learn in This Workbook

Four More Articles Editors Love – And How to Write Them, Book 6 is a continuation of Book 5. Book 6 looks at the four, more basic articles found in many Christian and secular magazines. You'll learn how to develop the individual formats that make up these articles.

- "How-To Write and Sell the How-To Article"
- "Writing Newspaper Articles and Mini Columns"
- "Breaking into the Magazine Market with Fillers"
- "Seeing the World—Writing the Travel Article"

Section I: Writing and Selling the "How-To" Article

"The more that you read, the more things you will know. The more that you learn, the more places you'll go." ~Dr. Seuss

Used in both the Christian and secular market, the How-To Article is considered one of the easiest to write. Let me show you how to write about what you know, find a solution to a challenge, or share an easier way to solve a problem. Use quality photos to sell your How-To craft article ideas to editors by showing the materials needed, the steps involved in the directions, and the finished product. Learn how to write in a sequence of steps, and give readers confidence in learning new information.

Personally, the most popular and easiest to write article is the How-To article. For the most part, people read for enjoyment, but also to learn how to accomplish something. They find it in magazines, on websites and in non-fiction books. Readers want to know how to save money on groceries, how to find the best doctor for the family, how to create a less stressful life, or how to live a better life. This is where How-To articles reach people by offering step-by-step guidelines and simple information.

Although easy to write, the How-To article still needs correct information presented in an interesting and entertaining style. Always use an interesting hook, good anecdotes, and solid examples. Photos are a "must" for showing the "process" and the "completed product."

Writing the How-To article can come from your own personal experience or from interviewing someone who has completed this project or excelled in the event.

As I consider this the basic or simplest article type, I suggest that novice writers begin with this type magazine style of writing.

As you begin, answer these questions:

- What subject do you know that you could teach others?
  1._____
  2._____
  3._____
- Is there a subject "you" want to know more about?
  1._____
  2._____
  3._____
- What have you learned you could share with others?
  1._____
  2._____
  3._____
- Have you discovered a new solution to an old problem?
  1._____
  2._____
  3._____
- Have you found an easier way to do something?
  1._____
  2._____
  3._____

Writing the How-To Article

1. Think of a way to solve a problem.
Example: How to Improve Your Marriage, How to Talk With Your Child's Teacher, How to Complete a Job Application

2. Self-Improvement Techniques.
Example: Developing a Daily Devotion Routine, How to Lose Weight—and Keep it Off

3. How to Build...
Example: a birdhouse, an outdoor patio, a sand castle

4. How to Make...
Example: A 3-layer cake (that will not fall), an award winning 4-H dress

5. How to Be...
Example: Five steps to becoming a better organizer, How to Be a Better Driver

6. How to...
Example: How to Cook From Scratch While Saving Money, How to Prepare a Sunday School Lesson for Teenagers

Advice on Writing How-To Articles

1. Know your market. Once again, writers must know the type of articles that are used in individual markets. Scan back articles—located online in the archives—or read the hardcopy edition. If you can't find the publication, request the company mail you a recent copy. Always offer to pay. As you read the magazine, look for How-To articles. If none are found, they aren't likely to start publishing them. It isn't your place, the writer, to suggest they change the format.

List 3 magazines that you would like to submit a query and later an article. Are How-To articles used in these magazines?

1._____

2._____

3._____

2. Know your readers. Knowing your readers makes all the difference in submitting articles that are published—compared to rejected. And how do you know the readers?

- Look at several (at least 6) back copies of the magazine.
- What do the articles tell you about the readers?
- Does the magazine provide clues about the income or social economic level of the readers?
- What is the educational level?
- Are the readers parents or young children, teens or retired?
- What do they purchase?

The answer to these questions gives you a profile of the person who reads your article. Will your topic meet their needs and be of interest?

Write several articles by changing the slant and lead. If you can't come up with a different slant, try *webbing.* If you're unfamiliar with this term for writers, write the topic inside a circle in the middle of a sheet of paper. As an example, take the topic "Family." There is no way you could cover this broad a topic in a 1,000-word article. So break it down into smaller parts. Divide and subdivide again. Webbing could look something like this:

Family
Groups: Parents – Children—Grandparents—Extended Family
Next, pull out topics that could be used as articles. Example, "parents."
Parents:
Sub-topics: Careers, religion, school involvement, sports

Children:
Sub-topics: extracurricular activities, church sponsored events
Grandparents
Sub-topics: baby-sitting, over-spending on grandchildren
Extended Family
Sub-topics: reunions, vacationing as a family unit, holidays

Choose a topic. Write down as many groups and sub-groups from this one word.

_____

_____

_____

_____

As an 8th grade student, I was assigned my first term paper. This first-year teacher gave no instruction on "how" to write such an assignment. So being a young girl who loved horses…that's what I chose. "Horses." I asked the librarian to help me find books on "horses." Soon she had a large stack of books on this animal. She asked, "Did I want information on farm, show, riding, or horses for breeding?" I had absolutely no idea! And this was for a 1,000-word paper! I had no clue how to begin or how to break it down into manageable parts. Hopefully future students had an easier approach to writing than I was taught.

3. Use one idea per article. Use the "keyhole effect" (when looking through the keyhole of an old door, you can only see a small portion of the room). Or it's often called a "snapshot approach" where you focus quickly on a short article. Another example:
Food – Diet – "How I lost 65 lbs. by eating one meal a day"
Health – High Blood Pressure—"5 Ways to Lower Your Blood Pressure"

Family – Young Children – "How to Introduce A New Pet to Your Youngster"

Chose a topic. Using a keyhole effect narrow the topic down into one main focus.

Topic:_____

_____

_____

4. Use your ideas to spin-off to non-competitive markets. As long as a local magazine or newspaper doesn't compete with another circulation—this is no problem. I write for several county newspapers and the editors are aware of this policy. Each week I email the same article to a number of newspapers. None of these overlap with the audience of the others. The article has to be generic enough and not include locations or places. Otherwise the paper would lose readers.

However, if each newspaper insists on adapting the article to its audience, you can easily insert words such as the town, county or places of interest. This requires only a few extra minutes of time.

Usually magazines that deal with these areas or groups of people do not overlap. You're not using the same article—you're using some of the research and data, but the audience is different. Change the title and focus, and you have a new article. It's always best to discuss this with any editor who gives you an assignment. Being honest and truthful are the only ways to gain the respect of others.

Example: regional, state, national and international magazines
Example: families, senior adults, parents, teens, children
List magazines that could be a spin-off for another publication:
1._____
2._____
3._____

I admit, I wasn't born with a *silver spoon* in my mouth, but I did inherit a love of turning something most people would discard into something useful. It was that "make-do" attitude, "use-it-up" or "do-without" approach to living that provided the *good life* I grew up with and enjoy to this day.

I see things differently from most people. Did you know a discarded 5-gallon plastic bucket can be turned into a garden container? Being a gardener, I take my scissors, shears, seeds, and potting supplies outside for a relaxing day of planting. Soon I misplace the shears. Now where did I put the scissors? And has anyone seen the package of marigold seed? Surely, there must be an easier solution. Then I spy the empty bucket! So if this idea makes my life easier, could it help other gardeners too?

Mature Living, a Christian magazine for seniors, published this article and photos (below).

A Bucket for all Seasons
By Carolyn Tomlin

Do you struggle with completing certain chores or projects? If so, combining the necessary equipment in one location might encourage you to complete your tasks.

Start by making a handy, attractive utility bucket to store everything you need in one place. Next make a list and assemble items needed for the project or activity.

Materials
- Five-gallon bucket
- Can of spray paint
- Adhesive tape (use by painters to protect trim work)
- Two plastic place-mats

Directions

Wash any residue from the bucket. Spray paint the bucket and allow it to dry. The paint covers any logo or printing. Decorate by adding a row of tape near the top and bottom.

Cut one place mat in half crosswise. Bind the cut edges with tape. Place the halves of the cut mat over the ends of the whole mat and sew or staple together on three sides, forming two pockets. Divide each pocket into two or three sections by sewing a straight seam through the two layers. Hang over the bucket so that one pocket is outside the bucket and the other pocket is on the inside.

Place the items needed for a project in each pocket. Place large items inside the bucket.

A bucket for all seasons will be a useful item that will help you stay organized. This project involves little expense and is easy to complete. Make one for yourself—another for a gardening friend.

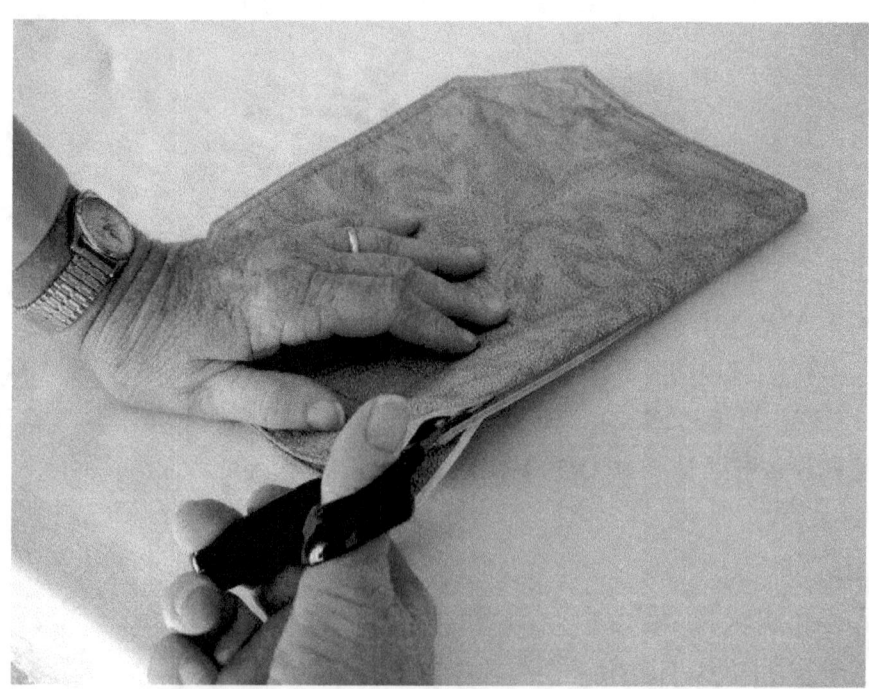

Collect these materials before starting on the garden bucket.

A 5-gallon bucket makes an attractive and useful container for organizing garden tools.

NOTE: I begin the article by involving the reader in a common problem gardeners share. In a chronological order, I list simple materials. Using a series of steps, I explain the directions. Last, I offer encouragement and suggest making another garden bucket for a friend.

After Reading the Article...

What did you learn about writing the how-to article?

_____

_____

_____

_____

_____

How could this article be written in another format?

_____

_____

_____

_____

_____

How can a How-To article help the reader?

By inspiring:

_____

_____

By informing:

_____

_____

By educating:

_____

_____

By entertaining:

_____

_____

Combining two family memories—a vacation and time spent playing games with our children—make up a How-To article. *Mature Living* published the article (below).

Title: Old Jigsaw Puzzles Frame Family Keepsakes
By Carolyn Tomlin

Instead of discarding those long-forgotten jigsaw puzzles stored on closet shelves, why not turn the puzzle pieces into a simple picture frame?

Materials
- Picture frame with glass and cardboard backing
- Jigsaw puzzle pieces (small pieces)
- Glue (suitable for cardboard or a hot glue gun)
- Photo and mat

Directions
1. Remove the glass and cardboard backing.
2. Glue one row of puzzle pieces around the edge of a picture frame. Building upon the first row, make a second and a third row of small puzzle pieces.
3. Hide all visible frame space. Select a mixture of light and dark pieces for a more pleasant appearance.
4. Select a photo appropriate for the rectangular opening. Use a mat if the photo is smaller than the frame.
5. Slide the glass, then the photo and cardboard backing, into the opening on the frame.
6. Use the frame as a focal point in a display. If you use a picture of a child or grandchild, add a few miniature toys reminiscent of that child. Of if the picture is of your spouse, add something that reminds you of a special event.

Jigsaw picture frames are simple to make and materials are inexpensive. Puzzles with missing pieces work great.

Include this craft project at your next senior adult meeting by asking volunteers to bring second-hand puzzles. A favorite photo, perhaps of a special occasion in their life, a child or grandchild's photograph, or a family home will make a treasured keepsake.

Caption: Using a hot glue gun, arrange puzzle pieces around the edge of a picture frame.

Insert a photo that reminds you of a special family event.

_____

NOTE: For a magazine that focuses on families, I suggested two items that bring back memories: puzzles enjoyed by the family and a riverboat vacation by the clan. It's an inexpensive craft and simple to make.

After reading this article…

1. As a reader, would you need additional information to complete the project? If so, what?

_____

_____

_____

2. Why would this craft project be one that children, parents, and grandparents could enjoy together?

_____

_____

_____

Write down the names of magazines that use How-to articles.

1._____

2._____

3._____

4._____

Check Your Creative Mind

In the next five minutes, see how many How-To ideas you can come up with.

1. _____   2._____

3. _____   4. _____

5._____   6._____

7. _____   8. _____

9. _____   10._____

Another How-to Article...

Another How-To article lists 5 topics as a way to make friends. This article (below) was published by *Living Light News,* a Canadian magazine.

Friends: How to Make Then, How to Keep Them
By Carolyn Tomlin

A wise man once asked a younger man to count the apples on a nearby tree. Although the branches were loaded, he finally came up with the answer. Now, said the elder, "Count the apples that could come from the seeds on these apples you just counted."

"Why Sir, that would be impossible. You can't predict how many apples will grow and thrive from all these seeds."

It's true about apples; it's true about friends. Do you know people who enjoy an abundance of friends—while others lead lonely lives? Learning how to make friends and better yet, keep them should concern everyone. Look at the following tips:

When you're smiling. Understood in all languages, a smile opens the way for conversation. Often called a lazy man's emotions, it takes 43 facial muscles to frown and only 17 to smile. Try this: walk down a street or in a crowd of people where you are unknown. Try looking the people you meet in the eye and smile. Before long they will smile back. Now apply this practice to people you know. Allow a simple smile to open the door to an exchange of ideas.

Friends take time. Ben Jonson, the English playwright, poet and competitor of William Shakespeare in the early 17th century said, "True friendship consists not in the multitude of friends, but in their worth and value." Friendship, when neglected, is like a vineyard without a gardener. Friendship requires nurture and care. It's often said that if a person has five friends—the same as the fingers on one hand—they are fortunate. Even one or two true friends are a gift from God.

Service above self. Used as a motto by many organizations, volunteering brings you in contact with people. Make a list of places in your community that need an extra hand. For example, sign up at a local school as a tutor, help with mail-outs for nonprofit organizations, serve meals in a soup kitchen for homeless people, or volunteer to greet visitors at your church. Put yourself where people gather. Be positive and so will others. Don't come in to make changes.

Ladies, gentlemen, and children of all ages. When P.T. Barnum welcomed crowds to The Ringling Bros, Barnum & Bailey Circus, he used this greeting. As seniors, we need friends of all ages. If you have grandchildren, take time for fun and educational activities. If no little ones are in your family, "adopt" a neighbor's child or one from your church. Go outdoors and watch clouds form as rain moves in. Catch the scent of a fragrant flower. Listen and identify bird calls. Touch the morning dew as it lingers on fresh-mowed grass. Bite into an apple—straight from the tree. It's a known fact: Children learn best through their senses. Could this apply to seniors also? God has provided us with these wonderful sources for learning. Share these simple pleasures with children.

A recipe for friendship. In 1936 Dale Carnegie wrote the best-seller, *How to Win Friends and Influence People.* Today this book and his program continue to be widely read and used by millions. Basically he uses these principles: Become genuinely interested in others, smile, remember their name and use it in conversation, listen, talk about the other person's interest, and make people feel important.
For more information:
www.westegg.com/unmaintained/carneige/win-friends.html

You made me do it! Have you been around people and something happens—but it is never their fault? They put the blame on someone else. In keeping friends, we must remain affirmative. Often this means we must ignore insults—just mark them off as bad manners. Developing a sense of humor and seeing the funny side of the situation not only helps us makes friends, but keeps them.

NOTE: *Living Light News* is a Christian magazine that pulls in a secular audience. Therefore the material must reach both audiences. The editors prefer a humorous, light touch with short quick-read topics. Quotations must be from those who are well-respected as a writer of the faith.

_____

After Reading the Article...

How is the article "Friends: How to Make Them, How to Keep Them" a different format in a How-To article?

1._____

_____

2._____

_____

3._____

_____

How are quotations used in the article?

1._____

_____

2._____

_____

3._____

_____

Can you think of another approach to using this type article?

1._____

_____

2._____

_____

3._____

_____

Guidelines for Writing Successful How-To or Make-Do Articles

Anytime you can encourage someone to take something that is no longer useful and turn it into a usable object, you've reached a reader. Or to take materials already on hand, and to create something new, you've added interest to your article. Look at the following guidelines:

1. Tell the reader where to find the material, how much to use, and the appropriate cost. By knowing the magazine and the reader, you won't write about remodeling an expensive RV when the family can only budget for a camping trip.

2. Include cost and time. Although prices vary from one location to another, you can show a range of from five to ten dollars. Or write, "not more than twenty-five dollars," etc. In addition, readers want to know the time required to do a project. How many people are needed to complete it in one day? Or, a weekend?

3. Include simple instructions and directions. Use short sentences and paragraphs with one idea in each set of instruction. Use bullets to divide material.

4. Use photographs or line drawings to illustrate your step-by-step project. Make a photograph of the items needed, then the completed project. Learn to make quality photos that are at least 300 dpi or work with a professional photographer. Enlist the help of a professional artist to create line drawings if needed.

5. Show excitement in your project. How does completing the project give you satisfaction? How can this project be shared with others?

Writing the Self-Help, How-To Article

Encouraging a change in a person is one form of self-help or how-to-be type article. Inspirational articles can be written in this format, such as dealing with a terminal illness of a family member, losing a job, a phobia, overcoming divorce—any depressive emotion brought on by a troubling situation. The difference between the inspirational and the How-To is that the reader discovers how to solve the situation.

The solution is that faith in the power of God is the answer. We seek this divine influence and trust our inner strength to help us overcome, survive, manage, or find the good life—if we will follow the article's suggestions. Research from writers who focus on these topics is needed. Document theories and methods used by others in helping deal with these human difficulties.

Outline for Writing the Self-Help, How-To Article

- State the problem. (The Lead)
- Mention possible reasons the problem exists. (Causes of problem)
- Offer five or six suggestions in an easy-to follow format for solving the problem. (How to change)

Look at the following How-To article, published by *Living Light News,* on surviving the dark days of winter.

Beating Those Winter Blues
By Carolyn Tomlin

It's that time of year when darkness arrives early and cold weather out-stays its welcome. Instead of wishing for spring and early daffodils, thank God for a cozy house and warm fire. After the excitement of Christmas, don't lose contact with the "outside world." Keep in touch with family and friends by staying active and happy.

Everything's coming up roses. Order vegetable and flower catalogues from growers. Resolve to plant at least one new vegetable and flower variety this year. Revisit those your grandmother once grew in her garden. As senior adults down-size, the large garden may be a thing of the past. However, large pots and a raised bed can successfully grow many blooming plants and tasty food items.

Create a Mind-Maze. Could you create a word-search puzzle from plants you recall from memory? Share your puzzle with a friend—either through email or snail mail. Sitting by the fire with a warm mug of tea, while combining letters into words, is a perfect way to spend a winter afternoon.

Get Ready, Get Set—Get Organize. I have a friend whose recipe file dates back five decades. Collected from mission organizations, church meetings, and neighborhood gatherings, these odd pieces of paper represent favorite foods prepared with love. Tied together with a couple of rubber bands, they hold memories of families and friends. Do you wonder at the method of organization? Every two or three years the band breaks and is replaced.

So instead of this lazy method—take a day and get those precious recipes organized. Place in a computer file or write them on index cards.

You Made Me Love You. Think back. Who are the people in your life who made a difference? A favorite teacher? A minister? A childhood friend? Perhaps you haven't contacted them in years. If you don't know their address, the Internet is a good starting place. Drop them a note by telling what an impact they had on your life.

Guess "What's" Coming for Dinner? Choose a day without snow and ice and invite a small group of friends to lunch at your home. Ask each person to bring a new dish—they can choose a meat, vegetable, fruit, bread or dessert. Encourage guests to tell something about their recipe during the meal. Make copies of the recipes for guests.

Walking in a Winter Wonderland. Pull on your boots, gather a warm coat and mittens, and take a short walk on a crisp, cold winter day. For safety choose a day without snow or ice. Breathe deeply. Let the cold air fill your lungs. Thank God for the beauty He has created this season. It's been said, "With less to see, we see more clearly." Bare branches give us glimpses of far-away horizons, hidden by summer foliage.

Those Far-Away Places. Maybe they're only a dream, but dreams can come true. This winter request some travel brochures to places you've always wanted to visit. Even if it's only arm-chair travel, you'll explore unknown territory. Call a friend. Maybe this is the year to purchase those tickets.

Find ways to warm your spirits while waiting for temperatures to rise. Rejoice in this season of the year and thank God for giving you time for these opportunities.

———————

In the above article "Beating Winter Blues" state the:

Lead_____

_____

Causes of the
problem_____

_____

Solutions_____

_____

_____

_____

Secrets to Successful How-To Articles

Understanding and practicing common traits of successful writing-to-publish include:

1. Learn the basic techniques for writing nonfiction salable articles.
2. Write about what you enjoy—what you do well.
3. Let your excitement in the project shine through in your writing.
4. Brainstorm possible markets that use How-To articles.
5. Deal with rejection in a positive approach.
6. Follow the guidelines of a specific market, yet add freshness and style to articles.

How-to Article Checklist

Depending on the type of How-To article you write, answer these questions:

____Identify the type of How-To article.
- Self-help
- Informational
- Make and do

_____ Did you provide step-by-step instruction?
_____ Did you show excitement in the project?
_____ Did you include cost and items needed?
_____Have you offered suggestions for change?
_____Have you actually completed the project yourself, or interviewed another person who has been successful?
_____Did the article offer encouragement to the reader?

Notes from Section 1:

Section II: Writing Newspaper Articles and Mini-Columns

"To learn to read is to light a fire; every syllable that is spelled out is a spark." ~Victor Hugo

Your local newspaper is a source for writers. Newspaper articles and short columns run anywhere from 300 to under 1,000 words, with 750 words being an average. Keep your eyes and ears open to events in your community. Stay ahead of what is happening, and offer to write an article. Editors need *mini*-columns to finish out a column in magazines and newspapers. You can supply these needs by writing "tight" and "bright" articles that are geared to the audience and magazine.

Many famous writers of the past and of those of the present started their career with writing articles for small town newspapers. This not only provided for daily living needs, but the writer developed a following of readers. After serving as an apprentice to a newspaper, the writer often moved into writing fiction or non-fiction books.

Two of my favorite writers are Mark Twain (1835-1910) and Ernest Hemingway (1899-1961). Twain worked as a reporter and a journeyman printer on several small newspapers. Hemingway worked for the *Toronto Star*. Twain's *Huckleberry Finn* and Hemingway's *For Whom the Bell Tolls* continue to be best sellers. Numerous quotes are attributed to both writers and are often referenced by other authors.

"The man who does not read good books has no advantage over the man who can't read them." ~Mark Twain

"Anger is an acid that can do more harm to the vessel in which it is stored than to anything on which it is poured." ~Mark Twain

"The world breaks everyone, and afterward, some are strong at the broken places." ~Ernest Hemingway

"I like to listen. I have learned a great deal from listening carefully. Most people never listen." ~Ernest Hemingway

Why Write for Newspapers?

Of all the markets for writers, newspapers may be one of the largest. A wide variety of opportunities exists for features, columns and fillers. According to one report, approximately 13,000 print newspapers are published today. Although some have closed, online versions have increased. And the plus side: most accept freelance work.

Writers have an advantage in writing for local newspapers. By living in the area, you know the people to interview and the calendar of events. Add to this, you can provide a human interest approach to articles that would otherwise be dry and boring.

Newspapers focus on the following:

1. Local news. Although regional, national and international news may be included, readers want local happenings and events, which is top priority. Newspapers, such as the *New Yorker* and *The Kansas City Star* reach a larger audience, and local news is not as vital.

2. Current and up-to-date material. As newspapers have a short lead time, their information must be timely. Print magazines have a longer lead-time, often months in advance before the issue is published. Daily publications have a short lead time, and meeting editorial deadlines is required. For weekly newspapers, the event needs to be within seven days before publishing.

3. Profiles about interesting people. Readers like to read about people! What do they do? How are they making a difference in the community? What hobbies, volunteer work, and lifestyles are they involved in that is unique?

4. Local sports. If you check small town daily and weekly newspapers, you'll see a large section devoted to school sports. Why? Readers demand this feature. Breaking into newspaper writing may be easier during the summer months when school is not in session. Editors need writers to fill those pages.

Check Your Local Paper

When thinking about these four areas found in newspapers, break the larger columns down into smaller sections. Look in your local newspaper for the topics covered. Can you add a human interest approach to the following? Did you find these areas?

___Animal and pets

___Food or recipes

___Celebrities

___Fashion

___Letters to the editor

___Lifestyle

___Opinion page

___Profiles of interesting people

___School news

___Sports and local athletics

___Religion and church news

___Travel

Differences in Newspaper and Magazine Writing

Competition between printed newspapers and online publications is part of the publishing business. Writers who offer a fresh slant on an old topic, find interesting people doing unordinary things, and develop an understanding of how the wheels turn in your community will find editors assigning their work.

1. Newspaper writing includes the 5 W's. Include *who, what, when, where and why* of any article. Newspaper articles include these 5 W's at the beginning of the story, often in the first or lead

paragraph. Magazine articles may include some, and sometimes all of the 5 W's, but they're added within the text.

2. Newspaper articles need shorter leads. Magazines may allow several paragraphs to develop the lead—newspapers need this information within the first or second paragraph.

3. Newspaper articles are usually shorter in length. Magazines may allow 2,000 words for a feature article. Newspaper writing is "tight" and "bright." Writers are usually limited to 500 to 1,000 words.

4. Newspaper articles promote current events. Most happen within seven days or less. Magazine have a longer lead time—time to publish the publication and be delivered by snail mail.

How to Start Writing for Newspapers

It's been said, "You only have one chance to make a good impression." Use your best communications skills and present yourself in a professional way when inquiring about newspaper writing. These ideas have brought in assignments from other writers. They will work for you, too.

1. If you live in a small town or community, make an appointment to meet the editor. If you've been published, bring samples of clips that would be appropriate for a newspaper article. If you are an unpublished writer, talk about volunteer services, education or career experience.

2. If you live in a large city or metropolitan area, email the editor or send by regular mail samples of your work, a writer's bio, and a query letter regarding a feature article or column. Ask what opportunities would be available for writers.

3. Know the paper and the columns that appear. An editor wants to know that you're familiar with the local paper. What topic is not covered that you can supply? Why would you be the one to write a column?

4. Become a syndicated columnist. It's difficult breaking into the syndicated business—but not impossible. It's been compared to "swimming with the sharks." Often when a columnist retires or moves to another paper, a staff member is waiting to fill this slot. Instead of being a syndicated columnist, start your own business by emailing newspaper editors the same article. Follow this rule: Tell each editor that the same article will be emailed to non-competitive markets and those that do not overlap in circulation.

Successful newspaper writers find a gap that is not being filled, and supply that need.

In the following newspaper article, I interviewed a family-owned store that started a used book business and rented textbooks to college students. The article, focusing on local interest was published in *thecityNEWS*, Sept. 2012.

Angie's Attic—A Haven for Booklovers
By Carolyn Tomlin

One of the best-kept secrets in Jackson, Tennessee is located in Hamilton Hills Shopping Center –a few shops down from Trees N Trends. Tucked into a row of businesses, the attractive book room provides a haven for book-lovers to browse used and rare editions.

On entering, customers notice the front desk made from stacks of books. "Such a creative display for a book room!" remarked a woman whose arms overflowed with mysteries, westerns and science-fiction. Another was overhead to say, "The place reminds me of Davis-Kidd—just a little smaller." Comfortable chairs, ceiling fans and hardwood floors invite people to browse through the stacks and make a selection before leaving.

Owners Denton and Angie Shearin, and Michelle Clifford, know the book business. Being a family-owned, independent bookseller, they specialize in used books, rented college textbooks, DVD's, CD's and more. Local authors share space near the front with new selections. At one time, they owned an on-line book service where customers bought from their web site. "We would go out, find books, sell and ship," said Michelle. However, they realized something was missing—and that ingredient was meeting the people who make purchases.

"Making the decision to open a bookstore was the right choice," says Denton." First we rented space on Parkway in 2009. Later, we opened the store here in Hamilton Hills. The location has made a big difference in people finding us. We believe that customer service is vital to the success of any business. We know our customers by name and they often request a particular book or author. If another customer brings in the called for book, we notify the person."

Another plus with Angie's Attic is that all three of the owners are readers. For Denton, it's science fiction. Angie prefers mysteries and popular fiction. While Michelle, being an English major, chooses classical literature.

College students save up to 75% off from renting textbooks instead of buying. With the ISBN, you can telephone, stop by the store or go online and order. A book usually arrives in 7 to 10 business days. At the end of each semester, either return the book to Angie's Attic or drop in the mail with a free shipping label. Go online to their website, AngiesBookAttic.com and check for coupons to use on your next purchase. If you bring in books to sell, they offer cash or in-store credit.

I encourage you to support local commerce. Angie's Attic is owned by area people. If the citizens in Jackson promote neighborhood enterprises, this will open the door for more small businesses to call our city home. For more information call Angie's Attic at 731-256-1769.

———————

Carolyn Tomlin is the co-author of *The Secret Holocaust Diaries: The Untold Story of Nonna Bannister*, which is available at Angie's Attic. She teaches the Boot Camp for Christian Writers. Email: Carolyn.tomlin@yahoo.com[1]

In the newspaper article above, why would readers want to visit Angie's Attic? List three reasons.

1._____

2._____

3._____

Write the 5 W's found in this article.

Who_____

What_____

When_____

Where_____

How_____

Check your local newspaper for these articles. Are they presented in a timely manner? Do they focus on local people?

- Travel
- Opinion page
- Lifestyle
- Sports
- Business
- Entertainment

_____

[1] Bylines allow the writer to promote their books without purchasing ads in newspapers and magazines.

Checklist for Newspaper Columns

_____1. Does the article have an original, fresh title?

_____2. Did you choose an interesting topic and one you're qualified to write? Newspaper columnists become known for one area.

_____3. What is your area of expertise? Is it humor, politics, parenting, education or other?

_____4. Do you feel the reader will identify with you from your experience?

_____5. Do you regularly read professional writers in major newspapers?

_____6. Have you sharpen your skills by identifying who, what, when, where, and how of newspaper articles?

_____7. Is your topic timely and focused on local human interest?

_____8. Do you have a calendar of events for your area?

Writing the Mini-Column

Shakespeare said, "Brevity is the soul of wit." This is good advice for those who write mini-columns. Ranging from 300 to 1,000 words, the article must have a take-away. Often called a *purpose,* the article entertains, informs, educates or inspires. Due to the short length, the article focuses on one small aspect of the topic. The mini-column is not the place to explain or give an in-depth discussion of the subject.

New or inexperienced writers often think short articles are easier to write. After all, you only need 300 words! Not true! Every word has to count. The writing must be sharp, to the point, and hold the reader's attention. With longer works, a writer will be forgiven if not every word commands the reader's attention.

Eileen Walter, a columnist for the *Wadena Pioneer Journal* says:

> I find that the experience of living helps me project emotion into my nonfiction. I've been in places and situations you would not believe, and held every kind of job. I write from these experiences in my column.

Life experiences aid in writing. What about you? What jobs, careers, volunteer work, or situations would be helpful as you write? List 4 areas.

1._____

2._____

3._____

4._____

Eileen's advice to new writers goes like this:

> Let your emotion get out onto the paper. Don't let well-meaning non-writers read your material and give "helpful" advice. Open up all five senses and "feel" the world through them each day. Even if you're bored-- see, feel, and file it all away for future reference. Later, when you least expect it, something you filed away will be helpful in what you're writing, supplying you with a subject for your article or column. [Barnhart, Helene S., *How to Write & Sell the 8 Easiest Article Types.* Cincinnati: Writer's Digest Books, 1987. p. 160.]

Finding a Story for a Major Market

It doesn't happen every month, or week, or even every year. But occasionally, I've written for a weekly tabloid that goes into 10,000,000 homes. *American Profile* is that publication. This tabloid is inserted into weekly county papers and small-town newspapers. Guidelines are noted in the *Writer's Market:*

American Profile
Publishing Group of America, 341 Cool Springs Blvd., 4th Fl., Franklin, TN 37067. Website:www.americanprofile.com. 90% freelance written. Weekly magazine with national and regional editorial celebrating the people, places and experiences of hometowns across America. The 4-color magazine is distributed through small to community newspapers. Estab. 2,000. Circ. 10,000,000. Byline given. Pays on acceptance. No kill

fee. Buys first rights, buys electronic rights, buys 6-month exclusive rights. Editorial lead time 6 months. Submit seasonal material 1 year in advance. Accepts queries by mail; include SASE. Responds in 1 month to queries. Responds in 1 month to mss. Guidelines available online.

Nonfiction. Needs general interest, how-to-interview. No fiction, nostalgia, poetry, essays. Buys 250 mss/year. Query with published clips. Length: 350-1,000 words. Pays expenses of writers on assignment. Must have receipts.

Photos: State availability. Captions, identification of subjects, model releases, true name required. Reviews transparencies. Negotiates payment individually. Buys one-time rights, nonexclusive after 6 months.

Columns/Departments: Health; Family; Finances; Home Gardening

Tips: "Please visit the website to see our content and writing style."

Query for American Profile

Note: After the editor requested more information, I wrote this extended query and was assigned the article "Perfecting Fried Pies" that appeared in *American Profile, 2008*. I've discovered a major publication may request additional material before a feature is contracted. And, on occasion, you have to break the rules in writing a query. This was one of those times.

August 31, 2007

_____, Editor

American Profile

341 Cool Springs Boulevard, Suite 400

Franklin, TN 37067

Dear _____:

Thank you for speaking with me yesterday as to the Flippen story.

For some people, like Jack Flippen, if it wasn't for bad luck, he wouldn't have any luck at all. He, and his family, believe that if life gives you lemons—make lemonade. Or, in his case—pies.

Jack, a cotton farmer from Troy, TN (population 1,273) didn't like growing cotton. When a salesman from Stark's Nursery came by and offered him fruit trees on credit, he took the offer. In 1953 he set out 600 apple and 300 peach trees—between the rows of cotton—not convinced the trees would make it. Jack knew about raising fruit and vegetables, as his family had been "tailgaters," selling off the back of a truck. And he and his wife, Diane, known as "Mama Dan" had several children to feed.

For several years, the trees produced and Jack sold fruit in nearby towns and folks even stopped by his west Tennessee orchard. But as luck would have it, a hailstorm in the 1980s knocked all the fruit off the trees. Disappointment set in again. But Mama Dan, who he calls the "brains of the outfit," said, "Let's pick them up, peel those apples and peaches, freeze them and make fruit pies." She tried the pastry recipe on family and friends that winter and her husband gained 20 pounds from eating so many fried pies. And, you might say, the rest is history. Today, they own and operate Flippen Fruit Farm in Troy, Tennessee near the tourist area of Reelfoot Lake.

The article may contain some of the following:

- Buying a concession trailer and making pies at local festivals. People stood in line for over an hour to buy a fresh-made pie. Sold 20,000 pies during a 3-day event in 2002.
- Dealing with failure. Three times in the last 56 years, the crop was 100 percent wiped out.
- Due to early spring freezes, they had to buy from fruit growers in southern Alabama.
- A glass enclosed kitchen provides visitors a view of the pie making process where they make 3,500 pies daily.
- Flippens ships to all states using an over-night carrier.
- Internet web site increased sales. Sold over 1 million pies annually.
- Family owned and operated. Three generations run the business. Everyone works in the field, hoes the grass around the trees, picks and sells the fruit.
- Suzie Flippen Hoover says, "Working with family is different. Some

days we disagree, but you get over it. For a partnership to be successful, we have to pull together. I would say we have found the American dream."

When I contacted you last summer about the Rock-a-Billy Museum and others, you advised me to keep trying. Since that time, I've read *American Profile* each week. I believe this story would be a good read for your audience. The Flippen story has not been covered by major magazines—only a small farm magazine and the local paper.

I'll email a digital of Suzie Flippen Hoover selling peaches. Always smiling, she knows the value of keeping customers coming back to her stand. I look forward to hearing from you.

Thanks for reviewing,

Carolyn Tomlin

Why this query worked

Often I'll choose a magazine with a goal of writing for this publication. With a circulation of over 10,000,000 --*American Profile* was one such magazine. Look at the following ways I addressed the topic:

1. Know the magazine and readers. The magazine published stories of small towns, in America, with people making a difference where they lived.
2. Network with the editor. I knew the editor by having submitted queries on other topics and reminded him of this prior contact.
3. Never give up. Although I had submitted other queries and they were rejected, the editor encouraged me to keep trying. If an editor takes time to offer this advice, take it and make it work. The first Flippen peach query didn't offer enough information to impress a committee that makes the assignment. The editor suggested I try again, giving more details. I did this immediately (within 24 hours) and emailed a fuller query. This time I received a contract. This was not the typical format for a query.

4. List topics that may, or may not, be included in the article. Show, instead of tell, what you will write. Can you paint word pictures of scenes you want the editor to see?
5. I wanted the editor to know I took his advice from a rejected query and read weekly copies of *American Profile.*
6. Digitals were included of one of the family members selling peaches.
7. Quotes from the family and those who bought peaches helped weave the article together.
8. This is the article as it appeared in *American Profile* Magazine, 2008.

Made in America Section
"Perfecting Fried Pies"

Diane Flippen, 74, feeds a ball of dough into a press in the kitchen at Flippens Fruit Farm & Hillbilly Barn near Troy, Tennessee (pop. 1,273). Leading a team of busy cooks, Flippen, known as "Mama Dan," then begins shaping the flattened dough into pie shells, before loading each with fruit filling and putting the pies into the deep fryer.

After the pies are fried and cooled, they're stored in large freezers, awaiting shipment to small grocery stores, convenience stores and individual customers across the nation. It's a process that produces 3,500 pies a day and more than 1 million pastries a year that bear the name Flippens Fried Pies.

Most of the fruit for the filling is grown on the 150-acre family farm, where three generations of Flippens have planted and tended an orchard of apple, peach, nectarine and pear trees.

While the Flippen family is famous for its delicious desserts, they never intended to venture into the pie-making business. Family patriarch Jack Flippen, 77, who began farming the land in 1951, says the pies were the delicious results of a natural disaster.

"A hailstorm in 1984 knocked off the ripe peaches," says Jack, who was unable to sell the bruised peaches on the fresh market. "I thought we were gone under." But his wife, Mama Dan, had another idea. Jack recalls her promising to "pick up those peaches, cook them and make fruit pies."

So Mama Dan did just that, spending an entire winter trying recipe after recipe with the help of Jack, who served as the taste-tester. "I gained 20 pounds that season," Jack says laughing. "Everyone that came by, she fed pies."

Eventually she perfected the right combination of flaky crust and sweet fruit filling. "It's tree-ripened peaches boiled down in taste, then fried in peanut oil," says daughter, Suzie Flippen Hoover, 50, of the family's fried peach pies.

At first, the Flippens sold the pies to friends and neighbors. Then, in 1988, they set up a booth at the Reelfoot Arts & Crafts Festival at Reelfoot Lake, a state park close to their farm, and sold about 150 pies. Excited by their customers' response, they bought a concession wagon and traveled the country selling pies at community festivals.

To help spread the word, Jack and Diane's son, Hayes, 49, started a convenience and grocery stores route between Memphis, Tennessee and eastern Arkansas. "I just told store managers how good my mama's pies tasted," Hays says, "and the rest is history."

Word spread about the dessert, and today Flippen Fried pies, which include flavors such as apple, peach, blackberry, cherry and chocolate, are the mainstay of the family business. While visitors to the farm can buy the pies fresh from the fryer, thousands of customers across the nation order the $2.50 pies and have them delivered by overnight carrier to their home. "I'll even sell one-half pie if that's all you want," Jack says.

In addition to the fired pies, the Flippens also sell items such as jams, jellies and cookies from Mama Dan's kitchen.

"All the Flippen children work in the business," Suzie says. "I pick, I plant and I hoe. I live in the orchard."

The family, which includes Jack and Diane's three children and their three grandchildren, is an important part of the business, Jack says. "Some farmers make the mistake of just paying family members a salary," he says. "Everything here is divided equally."

The result has been a family that's dedicated to making a great product.

Joanne Chambers, one of Flippens Fruit Farms' 25 employees, has seen that dedication firsthand. "We can't sell a bad pie," Chambers says. "Customers know what to expect. It's a small town, mom-and-pop business that Jack and Diane started themselves. They put blood, sweat and tears into making it a success."

Brenda Williams, of Jackson, Tennessee (pop. 59,643), has been eating Flippens Fried Pies for years. "I understand why they're called 'The World's Best Fried Pies,'" Williams says. "Other pies can't compare with the flaky crust and just-right filling."

Suzie Flippen, welcomes customers to her peach stand.

———————

Story by Carolyn Ross Tomlin of Jackson, TN.

(Note: Using a total of 668 words, I wrote the story of how an American farm family worked together to build a successful business. This met the tone of the magazine and readers. After the story was published, the Flippen family hired more workers –just to answer the phone and take orders.)

The Rewards of Being a Columnist

A writer friend says, "Being a writer is better than being a brain surgeon." People seek you out. They want to tell you a story. And they ask: Do you think I could write a book?

Once on a tour with well-known health care professionals, someone asked "what" I did? Before I thought, I said, "I'm a writer." For the next 10 days, I was cornered by numerous doctors who wanted to write their memoirs. And they wanted me to explain how to do this—in an hour, or less! But there are rewards. These are the most common:
1. I look for your column every week...
2. How do you come up with so many ideas?
3. We need a program for our next meeting. Could you come and talk about your featured newspaper column?
3. I usually enjoy your column, but this week—I have to disagree with you. In fact, I've contacted the publisher...

Guidelines for Writing Mini-Columns

1. Keep a running list of topics that can be turned into mini-columns.
2. Consider topics that will hold interest for a long period of time?
3. Practice brevity, instead of length.
4. Use feature articles as a spin-off for mini-columns. If rejected, break the feature into smaller sections and write individual articles.

5. Read columns from well-known writers, such as "Dear Abby," "Erma Bombeck" and others. However, be your own person. You are an individual and will have a unique twist to your personal writings.

6. Check the *Writer's Market* and *Christian Writers' Market* for magazines and newspapers that use mini-columns.

Mini-Column Checklist

___1. Did you write "tight" and "bright?" Did every word count?

___2. Did you stay within the word count?

___3. Did you use active verbs?

___4. Did you avoid over-using excessive adjectives and adverbs?

___5. Have you used a key-hole approach by focusing on one small event?

___6. Do you know the lead time if submitting for a holiday or season?

Notes from Section II:

Section III: Breaking into the Magazine Market with Fillers

"Reading is the discount ticket to everywhere." ~Mary Schmich

Do you have an amusing anecdote? What about a child's cute saying? Or can you supply a brief quotation that matches the tone of the publication? Let me show you how to find these markets that use brief fillers and mini-columns. I'll explain how to: Listen to conversations. Observe people. And come up with original thoughts that can turn your words into entertainment or *laugh lines* that bring smiles to readers' faces. Used for both the Christian and secular magazines.

The following filler was published in *CountryPlace* Magazine. The article idea came from "Big Red," an Irish setter, the dog that was very much a part of our family.

Trick or Treating Was "Ruff, Ruff"
By Carolyn Tomlin

When our children were of trick-or-treating age, they never failed to dress up and go door to door seeking candy treats. But when they rang the doorbell, the homeowners were just as likely to hear "ruff! ruff!" as they were to hear our children's cry of "trick or treat!" That's because our Irish setter, Big Red, thought he was just another one of the kids when it came to Halloween.

Big Red followed the children everywhere when they left our yard, and Halloween was no exception. He even got in the spirit by being dressed in a costume, much to his delight. His attire was usually my son's old boxer shorts—turned around with the opening in front for his tail to hang out, a necktie, floppy hat, and sunglasses.

As the children visited neighbors in our rural area, Big Red carried his own plastic pumpkin for collecting his bounty. When my son rang the doorbell at each home, Big Red always pushed in front of the group and sat patiently holding the pumpkin bucket handle in his mouth, ready for a treat.

Tootsie Rolls were by far his favorite, but chocolate chip cookies came in a close second.

While the children enjoyed their Halloween night out, my husband and I didn't have to worry. We knew they were safe with Big Red escorting them from house to house.

Disclaimer: Chocolate should not be given to dogs. It can cause illness and in some cases, even death.

Respond to the following questions from the filler.

1. A short article, such as a filler, needs one topic. What is the keyhole effect used in this article?

_____

2. What makes the reader smile?

_____

3. List descriptive adjectives or adverbs.

_____

_____

4. What words help you visualize how the dog might appear dressed in a Halloween costume?

_____

Many writers started their careers with writing fillers for publications. It's much easier to write the 100-word filler than a longer, 1,500-word article. Some writers make their living writing short, catchy articles that fill-up space between regular features. Not only does this type writing pay, you only need a creative mind, a little time, and some writing ability.

These suggestions have worked for me. Use them as a guide when writing fillers.

1. Know the magazine. Know the reader. You've heard this before, but I can't stress it enough for writers. Make sure you send the filler to the correct editor who handles this department. If unsure, call the 800 number or click on the "contact us" and email your request. By understanding the magazine, you won't send a women's makeup idea to a men's hunting magazine.

2. Review three to six months of back copies to become familiar with the magazine. What is the tone (i.e., funny, warm, historical, inspirational, etc.) and the target audience?

3. Know the submission guidelines. Find these by checking the *Writer's Market* or the magazine's website. With cuts being made for many magazines, the staff writes many of the feature articles. As a beginner, you may receive rejections from article queries, but fillers are open for freelance work. Space in a publication often depends on advertising and writers whose assigned work comes in short of the word count. If the editor has several of your fillers that meet the tone and audience of the magazine—your work has a good chance of being used.

4. Keep a folder of interesting facts. What topics interest you? You can add these topics to a file folder on your computer, or clip newspaper articles and place in a topical file. Do

whatever works best for you. Many readers look for short-read articles. Once they've picked up the magazine and read these and find them interesting, they're more likely to read feature articles.

5. Create a web of topics that interest you. For example, if "Families" are of interest, write that word in the center. Out from this, come up with sub-topics that relate to families. Such as: budgets, vacations, entertainment, pets, extended family, education, recipes and others. There is no limit to the sub-topics that relate to the main topic. If you're a new parent, share tips for helping an infant sleep through the night. Or, list 10 recipes for using hamburger in main meals.

6. Offer tips on your chosen topic. After reading a longer feature article in another magazine, this may trigger a completely different thought on the subject. Writer a couple of paragraphs and submit to the publication. Find a topic that interest you and write your thoughts.

7. Write fillers that entertain. Fillers such as this include: funny stories, inspirational thoughts, jokes, laugh-lines, poems, quizzes, word-searches, and others. Although information is most important, editors know readers like to be entertained.

8. Food and more food. Many magazines have sections that offer recipes. Check out fitness and nutrition, kid's magazines, hunting magazines (preparing wild game), campground recipes, feeding large crowds and many others.

9. Know the delivery method. Most editors request email submission, but a few still prefer snail mail. If this is the suggested delivery, include a brief cover letter and a self-addressed, stamped envelope (SASE). An editor wants to know you are familiar with the magazine.

10. The secret of success. Submit fillers, one at a time, to many different editors on a regular time-frame. Fillers are a quick way to make money and collect published clips. After an editor has purchased several from you, write a query for a feature article. Because fillers are short in length, do not

query. Paste the filler into the body of the email to insure the editor's computer doesn't pick up a virus. Always type the filler—never send a hand-written article.

Magazines That Use Fillers

Study back copies of magazines you would be interested in submitting fillers. List the magazine in the left column. On the right, list the type fillers used.

Magazine Title   Type Filler

_____   _____

_____   _____

_____   _____

_____   _____

_____   _____

_____   _____

_____   _____

Filler Check-List

___1. Have you kept an inventory of ideas?

___2. Have you produced an article that is "tight" and "bright?"

___3. Did you use a "key-hole" effect by covering only one facet of the subject?

___4. Is your filler like a canvas—in that it paints word pictures?

___5. Does the filler blend with the tone of the magazine?

___6. Does the filler complement the demographics (reader)?

___7. If you submitted a word puzzle, joke, inspirational thought, etc., has the magazine used this type material in a prior issue?

Notes from Section III:

Section IV: See the World—Write the Travel Article

"Travel is fatal to prejudice, bigotry and narrow-mindedness."
~Mark Twain

Painting a visual picture of people, places, and things, (and making readers want to go there), is only one reason to write travel articles. The other reason? *Traveling free—or almost!* Personally, I have written dozen of travel articles while touring the U.S. and foreign countries. And most of the time, the published articles paid part of the trip! You'll learn how to contact an editor before you leave home, steps to follow after returning from your trip, how to search for an unusual twist to well-known sites, how to use quotes from famous people from the area, and the value of using a *photo package* to gain the editor's attention. You'll also discover how one location provides *spinoffs* to a number of salable articles. And don't overlook *armchair travelers*—these people that want to read your articles, but never leave home. Enjoy this fun and exciting way to use your talents as a writer.

Do you think that traveling to faraway places is necessary to become a travel writer? Is it necessary to travel to exotic places? No, of course not. You can be a travel writer in your own community. Search your local media for interesting people who travel. Does the local high school take a senior trip? Will your church travel to a mission site this year? Realize these individuals from your home town have interesting facts to share about a trip. Also, these places will have a universal appeal to readers who live in other parts of the country.

Travel writers understand the fact that for readers to become excited about a location, the writer has to show emotion. Infuse your magazine article with genuine enthusiasm, excitement, and pride. In other words, show—don't tell. Let your language spark an interest in the reader that they, too, want to find the same excitement you found—as a writer.

Quotes on Traveling

Many well-known writers have written their thoughts on the topic of traveling. Collect quotes related to travel and weave them throughout your articles. Here are a few:

- "Nothing so liberalizes a man and expands the kindly instincts that nature put in him as travel and contact with many kinds of people."

  ~Mark Twain

- "The world is a book, and those who do not travel read only a page."

  ~St. Augustine

- "For my part, I travel not to go anywhere, but to go. I travel for travel's sake. The great affair is to move."

  ~Robert Louis Stevenson

- "He who would travel happily must travel light."

  ~Antoine de Saint-Exupery

- Two roads diverged in a wood, and I took the one less traveled by, and that has made all the difference."

  ~Robert Frost

- "Thanks to the Interstate Highway System, it is now possible to travel from coast to coast without seeing anything."

  ~Charles Kuralt

Travel opens the door to education. As a child, I credit my mother with making traveling part of my upbringing. Each summer, we took a weeklong vacation. Whether we visited the beach, the mountains, or spent time with relatives—Mother planned the route to include historical sites, state capitals, and homes of famous people.

It's a trend I continue today. In the last few years, I've toured China, Russia, islands of the Caribbean, Canada, and Cuba as well as many states in the U.S. Through traveling, I'm learning about the customs and culture of our world's neighbors. And in this endeavor, I'm finding many opportunities to write about these adventures. Travel writing can change your life. You'll never be the same after you visit a country completely different from your own. Use your five senses to capture these experiences. Then write the travel article and include photos showing people, places and things.

The following article on Russia was published in *thecityNEWS,* October 2010, after I returned from a 2-week trip to the country. Travel writing can also be used to promote a book. As the co-author with Denise George of *The Secret Holocaust Diaries: The Untold Story of Nonna Bannister*, I wanted to visit the places where Nonna grew up. Living in the Ukraine and southern Russia, Nonna had a happy life as a child. This childhood prepared her for the prison camps and the horrors of the Holocaust. The article follows:

Title: Visit Moscow and St. Petersburg: Russia's Historic Cities
Subtitle: Traveling the Waterways of the Tsars

On a trip up the Volga River, the water route of the Tsars, Moscow and St. Petersburg provide an historical account of ancient Russian culture.

*   *   *   *

The onion-domed cathedrals scattered throughout Moscow and St. Petersburg, fit Nonna's description of her Russian homeland as depicted in *The Secret Holocaust Diaries: The Untold Story of Nonna Bannister.* I had the chance to see these and other ancient sites that told the story of *Mother Russia*.

As co-author of the *The Secret Holocaust Diaries,* I wanted to walk the same streets, visit the Russian Orthodox churches, and capture the peace and solitude found in parks of Rest and Culture. Recently, I traveled with a group to Moscow and up the Volga River to St. Petersburg.

Russian Orthodox Churches
During the Stalin era, many of the Russian churches were closed and destroyed. Bells were removed from those left standing, as these signaled people to come and worship. In some small villages, only one church remained. However, some priests led a movement to have the church designated as a "state-owned" museum in order to save the buildings. Fortunately, many of these beautiful churches and cathedrals survived.

The Russian Orthodox churches are different from houses of worship in the United States. Icons depicting Jesus, Mary and Biblical scenes adorn the walls from floor to ceiling. No pews exist. People either stand or kneel. Void of electricity, candles provide light. After centuries of use, the icons and frescos suffer from the ill effects of smoke. With winter temperatures often -30 degrees and no heat, heavy clothing was necessary for warmth.

Tour guides point out the flat style of painting that allows the icon to be viewed equally by all, regardless of position. Also, the churches are not symmetric structures as the belief that symmetry is the enemy of beauty.

Moscow and Villages along the Volga
Considered to be the heart of Russia and a symbol of her greatness, Moscow is a major scientific and cultural city of over 16 million people. For centuries, Russian tsars and emperors, including

Peter the Great and Catherine the Great were crowned here in the ancient Dormition Cathedral. This act lends legitimacy to the power entrusted to the person crowned, whether coming to the throne as a natural heir or selected as a member of the ruling family.

If a visitor to Russia was only allowed one photo, it would be St. Basil's Cathedral (also called the Cathedral of the Intercession) in Moscow's Red Square. Symbolic of Russia, the structure was built in 1555-1561 on the orders of Ivan the Terrible to celebrate victory over the Kazan Khanate—a victory that united Russian lands and made Moscow the capital. Comprised of nine churches, the unusual architecture towers above other buildings at 47.5 m. A legend exists that Ivan ordered the architects, Barma and Postnik, be blinded so as never to repeat such a wonder elsewhere.

Red Square, with "red" meaning "beautiful" in Slavonic, rivals the most famous squares in the world. In 1812 Napoleon inspected his troops in Red Square, yet soon experienced a crushing defeat. Later in 1945, the Victory Parade celebrated the end of World War II with soldiers from all fronts participating. Vladimir Lenin's tomb, containing the embalmed body of the dictator, is located nearby.

Adjacent to Red Square stands The Kremlin, a word meaning "forests" or "trees." Dating back to the 11th century, this is the oldest part of Moscow with the first manuscript reference dating from 1147. Constructed of large, well-baked red bricks, the walls range from 5 to 19 m. in height. Eighteen fortified towers surround the Kremlin overlooking the Moscow River. Today, this central architectural ensemble is the center of government and politics.

While in Moscow, travel the city by means of the Metro. The "underground palaces" contain more than twenty varieties of marble, sculpture, mosaics and murals from the best artists.

Moving on up the Volga River, we covered a distance of approximately 442 miles, for the 14-day trip. Using a water route, Peter the Great dreamed of navigating Russian cities. By 1825 a canal was built linking the two cities, but the passage was not maintained as more interest was put into a railway network. In the 1930s Josef Stalin solved the problem of a shortage of water to the capital and trade travel by building 7 concrete dams and 11 locks on the Volga. Stalin's "Committee for Internal Affairs" monitored the forced labor from the Gulag (meaning jail) prisoners to build the canal. However, building dams and large reservoirs created numerous problems as thousands of acres of fertile farmland flooded, causing many families to relocate to unknown destinations.

Russian villages dot the banks of the Volga. In Uglich, we visited the remains of a 10th century settlement with the first record of the town dating back to 1148. Another ancient city is Yaroslavl, a town destroyed by the Nazis during World War II. Today, citizens have rebuilt homes, churches and shops by making and selling native crafts.

St. Petersburg: A City of Education and Culture

St. Petersburg, where you'll find European influences, has been called one of the world's most beautiful cities. One of the most historic places to visit is the Hermitage, also known as Catherine's Palace. Here, over 1,000 rooms display nearly 3,000,000 exhibits collected over two centuries and feature some of the world's greatest masters, including Rembrandt, Renoir, Matisse, Picasso, Rubens, Leonardo da Vinci and others.

In 1717, the Prussian king, Frederick I, presented amber panels as a gift to Peter I. Walls, chandeliers, and artwork were constructed from amber—a Russian precious stone. Destroyed during World War II, the famous Amber Room reopened in a 2003 inaugural ceremony, making it one of the highlights of the Hermitage.

Another "must see" is Peterhof, the favorite palace of Peter the Great on the Gulf of Finland. Known as the "Russian Versailles," the gardens and fountains form a Grand Cascade stretching down to the sea. Thirty buildings and pavilions are decorated with over one hundred sculptures. Designed by skillful engineers and architects, terraces and a gravity-fed water system form a symmetrical composition where the fountains begin at 11:00 a.m. daily.

For history lovers, Russia is a country you must visit. Exploring the ancient monasteries, visiting the icon-walled cathedrals, watching the ballet *Swan Lake* and participating in a Cossack folkloric show—contribute in a small part to reliving the times of *old Mother Russia.*

Sidebar: The Onion Domes of Russia
Visible throughout Russia, the colors of the onion domes have a special meaning.
Black – submission. Often found in monasteries.
Green – the Holy Trinity.
Blue – Mary
Gold – Jesus. Gold domes placed on top of tall drum-like towers also resemble candles from a distance
Silver – Indicate the dome is modern and has not been painted.

The number of domes also has a special significance.
One—indicates Jesus
Three – Indicates the Holy Trinity.
Five—Indicates Jesus and the Four Evangelists.

_____

Tomlin writes for numerous Christian publications. She is the co-author of *The Secret Holocaust Diaries: The Untold Story of Nonna Bannister*. The book is available at local books stores and on line at www.amazon.com

Photos Should Include People, Places and Things

Travel writing should spark enough interest in a place to make readers want to take the trip. Realize that travel magazines depend on good photos to sell the story. Often they are as important to the article as the text. For example, a recent trip to Russia included the following photo groups:

People: Find local people engaged in typical work. I look for workers involved in local labor. Or the elderly with lined-faces that tell their own story. Avoid a full-face profile so your editor will not need a model release to use their photo in a magazine. If this is a national U.S. magazine, and you have photos of unknown people in foreign counties, this is usually not a problem for the editor. Avoid any celebrities or government officials. Check with your editor, first.

An elderly Russian woman sells wild flowers gathered along the roadside.

Places: Photograph a sign identifying the location, historic sites, theme park, river or dam. What photos would encourage people to make a visit? Photos with an identifying sign or marker add authenticity to your article.

The Hermitage contains over 3 million exhibits and is a favorite historical site.

Things: Photograph local crafts, natural resources, native food, wildlife, plants and local transportation. After you return, photos help you remember who, what, when, where, and how of your trip. Also, by seeing the digitals in a chronological order on your computer, it's easier to match the day with the event.

A windmill and split-rail fence form a picturesque scene for this wheat field.

Before You Depart...

Your airline ticket is made. Check. You have lodging reservations. Check. Optional tours have been chosen. Check. Your passport, ID, a major credit card and travelers' checks are ready. Check. Is there anything else you're forgotten before you depart? As a travel writer, there are several items to cover before leaving home. These will make it easier to produce articles that can be turned into cash when you return.

1. Request brochures, maps and travel guides from tourism centers and the Chamber of Commerce. With so much information on the web, Google the place you plan to visit and print out items of interest.

2. What season of the year will you visit the area? Look on the web for seasonal events, festivals, parades, museum exhibits, and other areas of interest.

3. Know the magazine. (I can't stress this enough.) Look through several back issues or check the archives on the web by typing in the magazine's name in the search bar. Who are the readers? Age? Economic level? Educational level? What products do they purchase? Do you see stories of low-cost vacations? Senior trips? Career travel? Photos and advertisements provide answers to many questions. The article you submit should be similar in format and content.

4. Write several queries to different magazines as to where you will go, what you will see, how your article will encourage people to visit—or provide "armchair" reading for others. A sidebar could include a list of events during the date of publication or area restaurants for family dining. In fact, make the editor want to travel to this location!

When You Return...

1. Soon after returning from your trip, organize your notes, brochures, maps and photos. Follow up on queries you submitted and were given the green light to write the article. If any queries were rejected, write a quick thank-you note to the editor, thanking them for reviewing your idea. And mention that you will submit another idea soon.

2. Review your notes and write the article, using all the senses you recall. Stay within the word count. Editors have an allotted space planned for your article. If the contract calls for 1,200 words, don't send 2,000. Neither submit 500 words. Meet the deadline and if possible, email early. Guidelines in The *Writer's Market* give the preferred method of delivery.

Tips for Travel Photos

With the use of digital photography, you can make hundreds of photos without additional cost. When I first started writing and selling articles, I spent a fortune on 35 mm. film and development. I was fortunate to have 2 or 3 good slides from a 36-frame roll. To send by regular mail required packaging the slides in plastic sleeves, adding a cardboard backing for protection, and making a trip to the Post Office to weigh and mail. Then I purchased an envelope for return postage. The process was time consuming and costly. Fortunately, with today's digital cameras, I email photos along with the query. If photos can be part of the package, I always include about 12 shots. Photos add interest to your article idea. When an editor views quality photos, the contract is likely to follow. Sending a staff photographer to make photos of your trip is too expensive. Therefore, make plenty of photos, as you may not return to this location.

Develop your skills as a photographer. Some magazines pay

extra for photos; others, it is part of the package. Check the *Writer's Market* for guidelines. Cover shots can run much more than those inside supporting an article.

Look for those things that illustrate the senses. For example, in New Orleans your senses include: Sight - street cars for transportation, horse and carriage for hire; Sounds- Jazz musicians, Touch – metal gates; Smells –Waterfront, street vendors; Taste – local foods.

Sights - horse and carriage

Sounds -jazz musicians

Touch -metal gates

Taste – local food

Smells – street vendors

Use your own photos, if possible. With your own, there is no problem with copyright. Editors like to work with writers who can produce quality photos. If you do not have photos, use royalty-free photo services. Go to Google Images. Type the name of the photo to support your article. Look for those produced by a government or state agency. These are paid for by tax dollars, and can be used free-of-charge. You "must" give credit to the agency when using these free photos. Also, find those with the highest dots-per-inch (dpi) as these are needed for a higher resolution when printing.

Example, this is the process I used when searching for an invasive southern weed, called "pigweed" for an article in *Growing Magazine*.
Google – Google Images—Invasive weeds—Pigweed
Download the images to your desktop or place it in a folder by that name. Email to the editor with your query and later your manuscript. Include a caption.

Travel Articles Checklist
____1. Did you find a new slant on a well-known location?
____2.If this is an unknown location, did you include sufficient information to make the reader want to travel?
____3. Did you include practical information, such as the best route, expected cost of lodging, family-friendly events, best season of the year to visit for handicap accommodations.
____4. Did you fact-check telephone numbers and web addresses for accuracy?
____5.If this is a seasonal article, did you allow the suggested lead time?
____6. Did you include the five senses—always a part of every travel article?

As You Write...

Writing for the magazine market reaches thousands—if not millions—of people monthly. The number of readers a magazine writer reaches depends on how busy they want to be, plus the success rate of publishing your work. Consider these points as you write:

- Develop a passion for writing. Think how you can educate, encourage, inform, and inspire others.
- Realize that "writing" and "teaching" are similar. What you know, you pass information along to others. It's like a circle with no end.
- Realize that writing isn't about "you." It's about helping "others," and showing how God can make a difference in their lives.
- Ask God for guidance as you write to bless people you may never meet. Your words can impact lives that bring glory to God.

Notes from Section IV:

Appendices 1: Developing a Writing Career –The Seasons of Life

For years I searched for something to fulfill this creative energy that was part of my life. During childhood my artistic side flowed by designing clothes for paper dolls, and then moved into making doll clothes. Soon I was making all my clothes and even sewed for others. Like a woven tapestry, this thread of creativity was part of who I was; part of my every thought, part of my being.

As a child, books intrigued me. So did a new tablet. I recall the excitement when I sharpened a new pencil for the first time. Or opened the first page of a new spiral-back writing tablet. It was something about that fresh, clean page that needed words to fill up the lines. Even the smell of a new tablet was exciting!

As I moved into the teen years, I entered the state fair where I won blue ribbons in sewing, flower arrangement, and embroidery. By this time, I was making almost all of my clothes. In fact, my homemade dresses measured up to those in any store. Perhaps that's because my mother insisted the sewing be perfect. There was no room for "half-doing" anything. Mother often said, "If it's worth doing, it's worth doing right!"

Into my life comes Matt Tomlin, a young, handsome ministerial student. Marrying at age 18, I made not only my wedding dress—a beautiful long-white satin gown with a long veil, but all my trousseau—known as "going-away" clothes. I never understood why the term was used for leaving on a 3-day honeymoon. Especially, when we returned, we rented a small apartment only five miles from my parents' home.

Marrying young has advantages – and sometimes disadvantages. But looking back, I wouldn't change a thing. As a student-wife, I attended Union University with my husband. Matt served as pastor of a small country church. Driving over 2-hours each Sunday, taught us to trust in God in unseen ways. Somehow the tires on our old car usually got us there and back each week. Between the produce from my parents' garden, his parents pitching in, and a church pounding each Christmas, we survived. You understand the word "pounding," don't you? That's where the congregation brings sacks or pounds of food. Once we received 15, five-pound bags of sugar –plus, jars of canned green beans, tomatoes, jellies, and pickles. How excited I was to fill our empty cabinets with all that wonderful food! Once again, imagination helped out when a meal consisted of a quart of home-canned tomatoes and spaghetti. Meat was a rare item. God provided.

Throughout my young adult years I tried numerous hobbies, projects, and activities. Looking back, everything revolved around innovative ideas. I searched for something new. How could I use my creative talent in a resourceful way? How could I be inspired by the natural world God created? Fascinated by designing clothes for myself and our daughter, I scanned *Vogue Magazines* and window-shopped at the best boutiques for women and children. Flower design, using something worthless to others and turning it into a treasure for our home, became a creative endeavor. I enjoyed the challenge of using simple ingredients to make delicious meals. Creativity was at work—only taking different paths.

Finding Mentors

But with all these projects and activities, I was still searching. Then one day I read that *LifeWay* offered a Summer Writing Conference where people could learn how to write and publish. My husband, Matt, and I attended. There we met Bob Hastings, one of the speakers who later became my mentor. Bob was the editor of the *Illinois Baptist Paper* and was the author of many magazines articles and books. Readers will remember his *Tinyburg Tales*, a fictional place where all the women are strong, the men are good-looking, and all the children are above average.

Bob introduced me to editors and wrote letters recommending me for writing and speaking assignments. One editor was Charlie Warren, editor of *Home Life Magazine*. After submitting my first article to Charlie, he said, "If you will let me help you, I believe you will be one of the writers we call on regularly." Do you recall having an elementary teacher take a red pencil and make numerous corrections on your paper? Well, that's exactly what Charlie did. He cut it to pieces! It dripped red ink! I'm sure he spent several hours making changes and showing me how I could rewrite and edit. I'll never forget his kindness to help a new writer.

And yes, I did return home from the writing conference with two assignments. But I was the only one—I think. That's because during the course of the workshop, we were told not to bother editors and never to go directly to their second floor office. Well, as soon as the speaker spoke these words, I headed upstairs. There are times when rules are meant to be broken. This was the time!

Teaching as a Way of Helping Others

I often recall those dedicated teachers who patiently taught me the mechanics of writing. Spanning from first-grade all the way through graduate school, these professionals have made a difference in my life and the lives of others. Teaching is like a circle with no end. What we give to others—they pass it along. I owe them a debt of gratitude.

Coming from a family of teachers, my mother, aunt, female cousins, and friends, I, too, chose a career in education. After teaching kindergarten students in public school to being Assistant Professor of Education at Union University, in Jackson, Tennessee, I completed thirty-three years of professional work as grant writer for the Jackson-Madison County School in Jackson, TN. Although I was teaching others to write, I still searched for that special spark that wasn't part of my life. That is until I wrote and sold my first article in *Living with Teenagers*, a Christian magazine published by *LifeWay*. "How to Communicate with Your Teen" was accepted and published in 1989. Now at last, I was a published author and life has never been the same.

Creativity takes numerous forms. Like the seasons, we, too, change. Perhaps I wasn't ready to write-to-publish until I was 48-years-old. But I can't imagine my life without putting words on paper—now a computer—and using my original ideas to communicate with readers.

Recently a woman asked me how I wrote so many articles. My reply, "You only have to know the 26 letters of the alphabet and numbers 1 – 10 and you can write anything." Well, maybe there's a little more to writing than that, but you understand the idea.

About this time, I met Denise George at a writer's conference. Isn't it strange how God gives us opportunities and it's up us to take advantage of these events? Already seasoned writers, Denise and I took a break from the session and ended up on an outside porch. An editor had suggested I might like to meet this woman—whose name was Denise George from Birmingham. I looked at her—she looked at me—and we introduced ourselves. And from that time on, we've been best friends. God is good! He had a plan that would take us on a journey that neither of us could imagine!

Boot Camp for Christian Writers

Denise and I continued our writing ministry. Mine, mostly magazine articles, and Denise, books. People we met asked us questions, such as: How did you start writing? What makes a difference in receiving a contract instead of a rejection letter? How can I network with other writers and editors? How can I write to inspire, educate, inform and entertain others? How can I write to glorify God? Endless questions. Unknown answers that needed a response.

After asking God how we could help others know this passion that we possessed, we decided to start a writing ministry for women, called "For Women Who Love to Write." After several weekend retreats, men starting requesting that they attend, also. To accommodate them, we started our Boot Camp for Christian Writers, an all-day event where we teach writing-to-publish.

By this year, 2012, we've taught over 1,000 people to write-to-publish. Beeson Divinity School on the campus of Samford University in Birmingham, AL has generously provided support and space for our workshops. We are under the umbrella of the Lay Academy of Theology and promoted in Beeson mail-outs. In west Tennessee, Union University in Jackson, TN is working with us to offer Boot Camps for people in this area. Through various media, such as newspapers, radio and television interviews, we are contacting people. Churches sponsor those unable to attend due to limited finances. People telephone about future seminars. Interest runs high.

Each year, several Boot Camps are offered at Beeson. As the need for learning-to-write grows, other locations are being considered.

As we reach more people who have a dream of writing-to-publish, we pray that we can be an instrument in the hands of God. That we will give Godly advice, encourage our Boot Campers, and be supportive as they network with others.

Appendices 2: Example of a Writer's Bio

Writer's Bio

Carolyn R. Tomlin
5 Greenway Drive
Jackson, TN 38305
Email: carolyn.tomlin@yahoo.com
Web page: www.carolyntomlin.com
Web page: www.BootCampforChristianWriters.com

Carolyn R.Tomlin has been in the field of education for over 33 years. During this time she was the director of a preschool program, a kindergarten and elementary teacher, Assistant Professor of Education at Union University, and retired in 2001 as the grant writer for the Jackson-Madison County School System. In four years she raised over $5.5 million dollars.

Mrs. Tomlin has combined her educational career with that of writing and photography. Since 1988 she has published 8 books and over 3,600 articles in the secular and Christian magazines, including: Journal Communications, Inc. (Bowling Green, KY; Jackson, TN Magazine, Images of Bartlett, TN, Asheville, NC, Dickson, TN), *American Profile, Entrepreneur, PTO Today, Today's School, Growing Edge, Tennessee Magazine, GRIT, Early Childhood News, The Kansas City Star* Newspaper, *Woodall Travel Magazines, Bus Tour Magazine, HomeLife, ParentLife, Mature Living* and others. *The Secret Holocaust Diaries: The Untold Story of Nonna Bannister,* published by Tyndale Publishers was published in April 2009 with co-author, Denise George. Recent books include: *What I Wish I'd Known Sooner: Parents* and *Teachers*, available as an ebook and printed edition with Amazon.com. and Barnes & Noble.

As a regular monthly columnist, she writes the "Parent Section" for *The City News* (Jackson, TN); Senior column for *Living Light News* (Canada); "A Parent Speaks" for *The Baptist & Reflector,* "The Best of the Rest" for *Mature Living* and the "Home & School Connection" a newspaper columns for several area newspapers.

Tomlin is a frequent speaker for teacher/parent workshops and teaches writing conferences. During the 1990s she was an annual speaker or workshop leader for LifeWay Writers Workshop in Nashville in which she encouraged others to become published authors. As the co-owner of "Boot Camp for Christian Writers," she teaches seminars with Denise George on writing-to-publish at Beeson Divinity School at Samford University in Birmingham. A frequent speaker at universities, civic clubs, women's Christian groups and libraries, Tomlin combines travel writing while teaching workshops in China, Russia, and the Caribbean,

Tomlin received a B.A. in Elementary Education from Union University, Jackson, TN; a M.Ed. in Elementary Education with a concentration in Early Childhood Ed, a certification in Supervision and Administration from the University of Memphis and has completed all course work for the Doctor of Education Degree.

She is a native of Jackson, Tennessee where she lives with her husband, Dr. Matt Tomlin, a Baptist minister. They are members of First Baptist Church, Jackson. The Tomlins have two children and six grandchildren. A red Pomeranian puppy chooses to share his life with the family.

Also by Carolyn Tomlin

The following books, in hardcopy, paperback, and as ebooks, can be ordered and/or downloaded through amazon.com as well as other outlets.

Boot Camp for Christian Writers Carolyn Tomlin Writing-To-Publish: The Basic Foundations 2

The Publishing Opportunities That Await You! Section I: In the first part of this book, I'll explain the type of articles in both the Christian and secular market that need your manuscript, work that will educate, encourage, entertain and inspire others through the written word! Learn editorial techniques for publishing, how to break into those markets, get your message across, and earn extra $$$.

The Basics of Article Publishing for Print Magazines & Online Magazines: Boot Camp for Christian Writers (Volume 4)

Use these as guidelines to write your own article. As an added bonus, I have included enrichment activities you can do at home or with a writing friend. Practice these activities and develop your skills as a writer. The book also has pages to write down your thoughts and ideas. I believe that writing is a gift given by God. He gives us this talent and it's up to us to learn the mechanics of putting words on paper. A Bible verse that has given me hope is Isaiah 40:31: "But those who hope in the Lord will renew their strength. They will soar on wings like eagles; they will run and not grow weary, they will walk and not be faint."

What I Wish I'd Known Sooner: Parents

Do you ever wish the things about being a parent hadn't taken you so long to learn? This book is part of a series and focuses on the joys of being a parent. Bits of wisdom the author learned from raising two children are interwoven with prayers. You'll laugh, and rejoice in this role of "Parenthood." Section two, The Home and School Connection, offers guidance and self-help for parents as they deal with school-related issues. You'll find answers to Bus Safety, Making Friends, Peer Pressure, How to Talk with the Teacher, and other topics.

What I Wish I'd Known Sooner: Teachers

Part of a series, this book is written for educators. Included are bits of wisdom, prayers for teachers and students. Chapters are divided into areas affecting teachers, such as First Day of School, Open House, Bus Duty, and others. This series has been used in speaking to teacher groups, given as a gift and as a quick read for those who are able to laugh instead of cry when facing situations that arise in everyday life. Prayers give the reader strength and courage.

More Alike than Different
(story and coloring book)

By Carolyn Tomlin, illustrated by Ellen C. Maze

This is a story of Matthew, a young boy, who makes friends with children in his community from different cultures and ethnic groups. He soon learns that God made and loves all children and that we are all "more alike than different." Black and white line drawings provide a kinesthetic form of learning as children color the simple pictures.

The Secret Holocaust Diaries: The Untold Story of Nonna Bannister by Nonna Bannister, Carolyn Tomlin and Denise George

Nonna Bannister almost carried a secret to her Tennessee grave. As the only known family survivor of the Holocaust, she came to America after the World War II, married Henry Bannister and did not tell him about being a Holocaust survivor for over forty years. Hidden under her dress, her grandmother tied a little ticking pillow filled with family photos. In this pillow, Nonna kept her secret. It's a true story of a little Russian girl who survived because of faith in God, love of family and the ability to forgive her enemies. This award-winning book was Published by *Tyndale House Publishers.*

The following books are out-of-print but may be available on www.half.com, www.amazon.com or other outlets.

Teachers as Published Writers
A practical guide to writing and publishing for teachers. Readers will learn how to know the magazine market, understand the reader's needs and sell ideas developed in the classroom. Other teachers will benefit from your ideas across the curriculum. Published by *Judy Wood Publishing Company.*

From the Cat's Point of View
Written for cat lovers, this book gives a glimpse inside the mind of our furry friends. Can cats read your mind? Do they relate to your emotions? Read looking at life through the eyes of a cat to discover more about yourself—as well as that of your feline.
Published by *Judy Wood Publishing Company.*

More Alike than Different, (A children's story book)
Focusing on accepting multicultural differences, Matthew, a young boy meets the people in his neighborhood. Written as an easy-reader and as a listen-to-me book, children will soon be repeating the phrases uses over and over again. Published by *WMU Publishers.*

Mental Pause
Taking a humorous approach at menopause, the author describes emotions and behaviors related to this time in a woman's life. Published by *Judy Wood Publishing Company.*

True Tales or Tall Tales: You Decide with Denise George and Carolyn Tomlin

Some stories are just too strange to be true—or are they? Based on stories from the news and the writer's creativity, you will not know if this is a true story or a tall tale. Turn to the back of the book to find the answer. Written for upper elementary and middle school students. Published by *Judy Wood Publishing Company.*

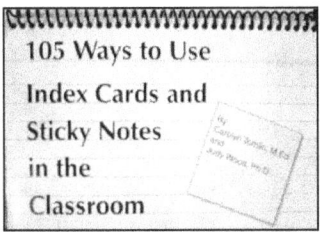

105 Ways to Use Index Cards and Sticky Notes in the Classroom, Judy Wood and Carolyn Tomlin

This book offers suggestions for using index cards and sticky notes in all areas of the curriculum—from reading, math, science, social studies and others. Published by *Judy Wood Publishing Company.*

A Parent's Guide to Summer Survival

School's out! The long-awaited summer vacation has finally arrived. For most kids, it's approximately 10 weeks (or 70 days, or 1,680 hours) each summer. For students, nothing could be better. For parents, what will you do with the kids all day? Instead of fussing, being bored, or having a "panic attack" try some of the great ideas in this book. Published by *Judy Wood Publishing Company.*

365 Email Messages for Students and Teachers (with Veronica Coulston) Make using the Internet and Email fun for students! Teachers find questions from the curriculum based on history, fine arts, sports, literature, social studies, science and other topics. Each day they email their class a question. The student must find the answer by using the Internet. Or, students can post the question for their peers. This is a fun way to learn, as well as master using the Internet and email. Published by *Judy Wood Publishing Company.*

The Tutor's Handbook: Math (Grade 2)

This helpful guide offers enrichment for students and includes: a sample tutoring session, creative tutoring strategies, reproducible work sheets and real-life math connections. Published by *Frank Schaffer Publications.*

First Steps in Missions, Vol. 6 with Tammie Worsham

Activities and ideas for Mission Friends and Teachers. This book offers fun and learning-based activities for home-schoolers, Vacation Bible Clubs, Christian schools and others. Published by Woman's Missionary Union

About the Author

Carolyn Tomlin has been writing and published since 1988. She has authored 14 books and over 4,000 magazine articles in magazines such as *Entrepreneur, Kansas City News, American Profile, Home Life, Mature Living, ParentLife*, and many others. She and Denise George are writing 14 books for the popular seminar, Boot Camp for Christian Writers. Her latest books are *What I Wish I'd Known Sooner: Parents, What I Wish I'd Known Sooner: Teachers* and *More Alike Than Different* (a story and coloring book for children.). Carolyn is married to Dr. Matt Tomlin, a Southern Baptist pastor. They have two adult children, Cindy Tomlin Coulston and Kevin Tomlin and six grandchildren.

You may contact Carolyn Tomlin at:
Carolyn's email address: Carolyn.tomlin@yahoo.com
Web Page: www.carolyntomlin.com
For writers: http://christianwritersbootcamp.blogspot.com
Beeson's website:
http://www.beesondivinity.com/bootcampforchristianwriters

Boot Camp for Christian Writers®

Boot Camp for Christian Writers® is a no-nonsense, basic, information-packed, series of all-day, one-day seminars that educate and equip Christian writers to write clearly, communicate effectively to a chosen audience, professionally approach magazine editors and book publishers with good ideas, and get articles and books published!

Founded in February, 2009, by Denise George and Carolyn Tomlin, Boot Camp for Christian Writers® is based on Colossians 3:12-17 and (Col. 3:23-24): "Whatever you do, work at it with all your heart, as working for the Lord, not for men... It is the Lord Christ you are serving."

George and Tomlin keep in close touch with their Boot Campers through email, and are available to answer questions, give advice, etc. Boot Campers can communicate with each other through the Boot Camp FaceBook Page. The Boot Camper Blogspot provides regular information on writing, tips, publishing trends, current writing news, photos, etc.

George and Tomlin teach using three modes of learning:

1. <u>Visual:</u> They offer the latest in technology with creative PowerPoint and KeyNote presentations;
2. <u>Auditory</u>: They present information in a comfortable classroom-style setting, and give question & answer opportunities after each seminar;
3. <u>Kinesthetic</u>: They provide printed handout materials to go along with their presentations, as well as personally-written books (like this one) that participants can purchase

to gain deeper understanding, further information, and self-learning exercises to use at home.

Hundreds of people have already participated in these information-packed seminars! The seminars are exciting and fun, and writers enjoy meeting each other and comparing ideas! Our Boot Campers are writing confidently, contacting editors with magazine and book ideas, selling articles to magazines, and receiving book contracts from major publishers! They are also learning how to self-publish and promote their books to the world! Attend one of the Boot Camp for Christian Writers® seminars and become a lifetime member of the "Family of Christian Writers."

Happy writing and may God bless you!

~ Carolyn Tomlin

Your Seminar Notes: